PERSPIRATION
PRINCIPLES

Howard A. Tullman

Perspiration Principles XX
Copyright © 2017 by Howard A. Tullman. All rights reserved.

No part of this publication may be reproduced, stored in a retrieval system or transmitted in any way by any means, electronic, mechanical, photocopy, recording or otherwise without the prior permission of the author except as provided by USA copyright law.

Published in the United States of America
For bulk orders, please contact info@blogintobook.com

Cover design portrait courtesy of Matthew Cherry
Perspiration Principles logo designed by James "Red" Schmitt
Special Thanks to Lakshmi Shenoy and Claudia Saric

To purchase more volumes of The Perspiration Principles, please visit:
BlogIntoBook.com/tullman/

To purchase "Tullman on Company Culture," please visit:
BlogIntoBook.com/companyculture/

DEDICATION

Sitting down every week to write something that will be meaningful and ideally of lasting value to others is a lot like setting out to start a new business. Sometimes there's a germ of an idea; sometimes it's an emotional reaction or other driver; or perhaps it's just a problem or situation that needs to be addressed. And occasionally you simply want to see things change and no one else is stepping up to the plate to make that happen.

You can't know how hard, long or costly (in many ways) the journey will be and there are no guarantees that anything good will ever come of your efforts, but you know for certain that nothing will ever happen if you don't get the process started and try. It's a lonely path and every bit of encouragement, assistance and support that you find along the way makes the job a little easier and slightly more likely to succeed.

I hope that these books will be my modest contribution to your success and to the well-worn and tattered bag of hopes and dreams which we call entrepreneurship.

CONTENTS

There's Never A Great Time To Go 7
Forget Failing Fast: Fail Forward 13
Build On Your Installed Base 17
Investors Are Losing Patience With Pivots 21
Scale Smart – Take Your Time – Pick Your Spots 27
Where Will Your Business Be When The Music Stops? 33
Don't Blame The Data For The Debacle 39
Make Your Meetings "Crisp" Or Forget Them 43
Wise Words From The Witch In Wicked 47
The Poor I.T. Guys Can Only Tie 51
About The Author 55

THERE'S NEVER A GREAT TIME TO GO

There have been a lot of prescriptive articles written over the last few years (mostly by academics and other people who haven't been there themselves) about the critical (and often ignored or overlooked) need for succession planning in large companies – especially at the level of the most senior management. I've seen massive notebooks at some big businesses that detail the candidates and the replacement process for practically every member of the senior management team.

On the other hand, apart from the occasional VC who insists on key man insurance as an investment condition, there's been very little discussion or literature about this issue in the startup world. Given how single-threaded so many startups are, you'd think this topic would be much more top of mind than it is.

It's clear that there's never a perfect moment to talk to the founding CEO of a startup about replacement, succession or making a prompt and graceful exit (even when everyone basically agrees that it's essential to moving the business to the next plateau) or about him or her being "kicked upstairs" to a board position or an advisory role, but treating the entire issue like it's a taboo subject doesn't make any sense at all. And yet, it's pretty much the ways things are and have always been. As many businesses as I have been a part of and as many times as I've addressed these issues as a Board member, it never seems to be a clear or easy process.

I think this is mainly for three reasons: (1) the incumbent CEO never wants to discuss stuff like this – it's just like talking about your will or your funeral plans with your wife or kids; (2) most VCs would tell you (if they were being remotely honest) that, in 75% or more of the cases where the company is wildly successful, they totally believe that they're going to have to fire/replace the CEO anyway so they'll worry about it down the road; and (3) it's too early in the company's brief lifetime to date to be discussing these kinds of "negative" ideas and concerns. We don't want to scare the troops or the investors. I call this last consideration the "let's rob the train first before we worry about splitting up the loot" mindset.

But the truth is that - no matter how unpleasant the topic may be - it's a good idea for the CEO when the time is right to get ahead of the pack and actually try to initiate and direct some of these discussions before they take on a life of their own and he or she becomes – at best - an interested bystander to the process. Boards rarely directly broach subjects like this without a precipitating event or a firm push or incentive from someone and it's almost always better to be the one making things happen than the one watching things happen – especially when they're happening to you.

But of course the hardest question in this process really isn't "who's next?" – the critical question is "when is the time right?" to start thinking about making at least a plan and maybe even a change. Interestingly enough, INC. Magazine's owner, Joe Mansueto, just stepped out of his CEO role at Morningstar – a company that he founded more than 30 years ago. He didn't wait to be asked or to be pushed – he knew that for him (and I imagine for the business as well) that the time was right. I've known Joe for decades, but – just to be clear – I haven't spoken to him about his decision and none of

Perspiration Principles XX

the considerations I discuss below should be attributed or assumed to have had any role in his choices.

How will you know when the time is right to at least start talking about the subject? Even if you think it's early (or never gonna happen to you), it's a good idea to know some of the internal signs and some of the emotional signals that will help you decide whether and when it's appropriate and smart to think about succession issues and your eventual (and hopefully consensual) decision to move on. I've talked to maybe a dozen serial entrepreneurs over the last couple of months specifically on this subject and, of course, I've been through the process many times myself and it's pretty clear that the inventory of emotions and concerns is fairly common. Here are the ones that I've seen and heard time and time again.

(1) When it feels more like an exhausting job than an exciting journey.

I've always thought it was stupid to ask an entrepreneur whether he or she is having "fun". Building a new business is a whole lot of things, but anyone who's lived through it won't tell you that it was a lot of fun. It's challenging, stimulating, overwhelming at times, and certainly satisfying when you succeed, but it's not a lark. When you're actively unhappy at the end of a long day instead of just being beat, it's time to think about beating it.

(2) When it feels more like pulling the wagon than leading the charge.

Leading people is always a challenge and it helps a bunch to have the right people on your team. But after you've shown them the vision and the path, in the best businesses, the burden's on them to move the ball forward. Trying to drag a disinterested division down the road or carry a "care less" crew on your back is just too much work for anyone to try to do alone. Begging your people to believe is a waste of breath. Find new people or a better place to be. You can't push a rope.

(3) When no one, but you is interested in what's new or what's next.

Businesses that don't keep raising the bar and getting better every day start dying. It's that simple, but that doesn't mean that it's easy to encourage everyone to keep one eye on the future. People inside your business are always reluctant to change or to part with what they see as working "just fine" for them. But meanwhile the rest of the world is trying to eat your lunch. This isn't about some fixation on always seeking the newest shiny object or buying the best new whatever – whether you need it or not. It's about living in a world where change is the only constant.

(4) When the process becomes more important than the business's progress.

Nothing is more heartbreaking for a true entrepreneur than watching bullshit bureaucracy slither its way into the business. Punctuality comes to trump productivity. Rules and regulations get in the way of real results. People prefer peace and quiet over progress. Hurt feelings are more important than hard facts. And too many crave consensus and the lowest common denominator over the chaos of creativity and new challenges.

Perspiration Principles XX

(5) When the conversations are about imitation rather than innovation.

If the best your business can do is just a little bit better or cheaper or faster, you won't be in business much longer. Thinking small and aiming low are self-fulfilling prophecies. And if I can write down a simple set of rules and instructions to do the lion's share of your business, a machine or a robot will be taking your place a couple of weeks from tomorrow. The future isn't going to be incremental – it's going to be radical - and the businesses that want to grow and survive will need to make a demonstrable difference in and add real value to people's lives. Design will be important, but not protectable or proprietary, because the web lets the whole world know what you're thinking and doing in an instant. Speed, impact and exemplary execution will be everything.

(6) When everyone's talking about better safe than sorry.

If all the talk is about saving the business's bacon and securing the status quo instead of the setting the curve and shooting for the stars, you're on the wrong escalator and headed in the wrong direction. You can't save your way to success; you can't steal second base with one foot on first; and, if we knew in advance how all these things were gonna work out, they probably wouldn't be worth doing in the first place. The caterpillar is safe in the cocoon, but it's the butterfly that's beautiful. The best businesses are richly rewarded for taking the greatest risks (not gambles, but calculated risks) and playing it safe today is the riskiest thing you can do.

(7) When you spend more time looking over your shoulder than over the next hill.

It's important to cherish and celebrate the past as long as you don't live in it. You can't change it; you won't forget it or get over it; and the very best that you can hope for is to avoid making the same old mistakes again. But the worst mistake of all is to use the past as an excuse for not moving forward or as a place to hide from an uncertain future. The best entrepreneurs run toward their fears, not away from them.

And, just to be clear, since the most critical choices are the ones we make with our hearts rather than our heads, you'll know it's time to go when your fears are greater than your dreams.

FORGET FAILING FAST: FAIL FORWARD

I'm so tired of regularly reading about and constantly being lectured on the virtues of failing fast that I'm beginning to wonder whether the phrase is an embedded Swift Key on mobile keypads or a built-in slide which is automatically inserted into PowerPoint and Keynote presentations. But, as I've said many times in the past, there's no fun in failing (See http://www.inc.com/howard-tullman/who-said-failure-was-fashionable.html) and it's no badge of honor to lose although I don't think that - for young entrepreneurs - it's really a case of losing in any event – because, even if you don't win, you learn a great deal as long as you're willing to listen.

Just remember that there's nothing noble about noble failures and that even the grandest failures aren't really fatal – they're just opportunities to start again – better and smarter. The truth is that you'll absolutely learn much more from your failures than your successes although it won't feel nearly as good. And, you never want to quit too soon because, in the startup world, almost everything looks like a failure in the middle. This is why perseverance is so crucial. Things always look grimmest right before success breaks through.

So, I'd like to retire the phrase "fail fast" and replace it with something that to me is a lot more descriptive of the whole experience and the smart way to look at the process. It's not ultimately about how quickly you fail, it's all about the education, the take-aways and specifically about the mistakes you hopefully won't make again. So instead of making sure that you are failing fast, my suggestion is that you try to "fail forward" when things are headed downhill. Learn and gain in the process. Brene Brown says failure is an "imperfect" word because it's never the end of the story if you're smart. Failures turn into lessons and lessons make you better going forward and somewhat more likely to succeed the next time around as long as you're a good listener. (See http://www.inc.com/howard-tullman-3-tips-from-brene-brown-about-failing-brilliantly.html)

Failing forward has all the virtues of failing fast - an awareness of opportunity costs - the ancient wisdom of "stopping the digging" when you find yourself deep in a hole - and an understanding of how seeking the cure for no known disease or working desperately on solutions for non-existent problems is such a sad waste of your energy and scarce resources. But an important distinction is that the idea of failing forward always looks ahead - gets you right back up on the horse again - and builds on the useful and valuable experiences of your prior attempts. In addition, if you handle the wind-down like a pro, you will actually make it much more likely that your next deal will be easier to get done because even failing well is an art. (See http://www.inc.com/howard-tullman/failure-happens-four-ways-to-do-it-well.html)

It's almost never about a clean sweep or a complete restart - there are too many babies in the bath water to just toss the whole thing out the window. It's always an iterative process with lots of triage included. You want to preserve what worked (remembering that someone spent a lot of time and money on your last adventure), you definitely want to hang on to the people who put their hearts and souls into the program, and you want to be humble and smart enough to carefully determine what went wrong and why. Just a word to the wise about that last idea - in the vast majority of cases - it will emerge that what bit you in the ass wasn't just something you weren't good enough at or something that you found out that you didn't know how to do - it will be something that you didn't even know that you didn't know (or hadn't thought about) that made all the difference.

The lesson here is that it's the careful research and the customer investigation - the stuff you do <u>before</u> you start – that, in the end, will turn out to have the greatest impact on the success of the business because real demand and customers are the whole ballgame. Everything else you can hire, fire, fix or improve as the battle progresses, but, if no one wants what you're selling, there's no there there.

BUILD ON YOUR INSTALLED BASE

I have been saying for at least 30 years now that the most attractive (and profitable) customers any business can have are the ones that you already have in house. It's more important to deepen your connection to your existing customers than to spend a lot of time and money trying to figure out why certain customers left. After all, while you might learn some things from the process, you can't really water yesterday's crops and, in any case, it feels a little too much to me like crying over spilt milk. Extract the necessary lessons, fix what can be fixed, and move forward.

Good existing customers get better and more valuable over time (increased spend, referrals, lower maintenance costs, etc.) and they represent the absolutelylowest-hanging fruit for additional incremental business (product and services add-ons, extensions, new offerings, service plans, etc.) as well as the greatest and easiest opportunity to increase your share of their total spend. (See http://www.inc.com/howard-tullman/why-knocking-on-old-doors-is-the-best-sales-strategy.html.)

So it's absolutely critical to do everything you can to hang on to your good customers and clients. Nothing is more important to your bottom line than preventing customer attrition and avoiding churn. If you can't do this, and you're spending a fortune on the front end to pull in new customers while you're losing them out the back, your company's going nowhere fast. It's like kissing your sister or as Yogi Berra used to say about his road trips: "We're lost, but we're making good time." The truth is that, if you're losing existing customers as quickly as you adding new ones, you're not making or building anything – you're just treading water – and once you run out of money, they make you go home.

The name of the long and winning game is to "own" your customers for life and to exceed their expectations throughout your relationship with them. Today we have the tools and the data concerning virtually all of our customers which should permit us to totally manage our relationships with them if we invest the time and money to look at the available information and – most importantly – if we know what we are looking for. Everything in life happens on a continuum (or a series of cycles) and your job is to monitor your customers' timelines and jump in at the appropriate junctures (long before the competition is even in the game) to make the next connection and the next sales.

When you're already in their wallet, you can absolutely work wonders. And when you're already connected to them through low-cost digital marketing and communication channels, assuming you haven't abused the privilege or their patience, you have an inexpensive and very direct channel to reach out to them with customized, personalized and timely offers consistent with their prior activities, past purchases, and interests. It's a marketer's dream scenario and it's the very essence of what I call "smart reach". (See http://www.inc.com/howard-tullman/to-sell-more-your-marketing-must-embrace-smart-reach.html.)

Part two of this process is making sure that you stay out in front of the customers and aggressively anticipate their desires, demands and requirements so that the offers you make to them make sense. As Steve Jobs used to say, they may not even know what they want and it's your job to entice, excite and encourage them in those next directions. If you do it well and consistently, the customers may never re-enter the competitive marketplace since you are effectively and pre-emptively satisfying their needs. (See http://www.inc.com/howard-tullman/keep-your-customers-by-thinking-ahead-of-them.html.) Today, I think there's probably no better example than the Amazon Dash buttons which permit on-site, as-needed, immediate re-ordering capability right in the consumers' homes at the place and precise time when they need to replenish or replace essential supplies. Be there when they want to buy.

The job of staying ahead of your customers is equally true whether you think you are selling a product or a service. The smartest operators know that every business is really a service business today because the real nature of every business is that it's always about making the next sale, managing the next interaction or event, delivering an uninterrupted stream of service, etc. You never want the customer "to come up for air" because if he or she does re-enter the marketplace and starts shopping around, your job becomes a million times harder.

So the ongoing task and the critical questions are always the same – how do I know when to act and how do I pre-empt/intercept the customer at exactly the right times in our relationship? The answer is actually easier than you would think because - even though the start and stop points on the cycle may vary by customer - at some definable and determinable point, every customer will move through the same cycle. You just have to understand and learn how to measure and manage the cycles.

The basic cycles are pretty much just extensions of human nature. It's a process that we are all already familiar with and living through every day ourselves. The five primary phases are:

Desire Leading to **Decision**
Action Leading to **Satisfaction**
Boredom Leading to New **Desire**

We want it, we buy it, we love it for a while, we get tired of it, and we want something new. Sound vaguely familiar. Well, here's a flash, this is a process that every single one of your customers is going through right now. Your job is to figure out who's where in which phase of the cycle. It's important to understand that the cycles are going to vary dramatically depending on a variety of important considerations and they will vary from industry to industry as well.

Some of the variables which will impact the types and durations of the cycles (but not the fundamental stages or phase within the cycle) include: (1) how large and financially/emotionally important is the transaction; (2) how often is a transaction likely to occur and what other connections/interactions with the customer will take place between transactions: and (3) how easy is it for the customer to change vendors, services or products and how readily available are competitive offerings?

But, regardless of a given cycle's duration, there are similar cycles to be identified, tracked and managed in every business and properly managed, these cycles are the keys to keeping your customers for li

INVESTORS ARE LOSING PATIENCE WITH PIVOTS

There's no polite or easy way to say this, but winter is on its way in more ways than one. It's getting tougher and tougher for startups caught in the lukewarm limbo between ideas and invoices to get their early backers to up their bets especially when it's not clear that they've found a viable business model and/or a way to stop the bleeding sooner rather than later. Too many pivots with too little to show for the dollars down the drain and pretty soon no one wants to hear your "someday soon" story or your next grand plan. (See http://www.inc.com/howard-tullman/you-can-pivot-but-you-should-never-twirl.html.) And if you're not even breaking even, no bank will look twice at your business or your balance sheet. This change isn't restricted to the unicorpses in the Valley; it's going on in every village where waves of wishful thinkers are starting to wonder what hit them.

My sense is that the smart investor conversations taking place today aren't very often about the company going big for the gold or about the current investors doubling down so some startup can shoot for the stars. These increasingly cranky chats are less about excitement and enthusiasm and much more about ennui and possible exits. Because the two things that some early investors and every VC understands are sunk costs and opportunity costs.

While the entrepreneur is sweating survival; the investors are trying to decide whether their incremental dollars would be better spent on a new deal elsewhere. These are the days when the easy money gets hard. Those great gluten-free sugar cookies (from the hip new bakery down the block that just shut its doors) are tasting more like ashes in their mouths and they're asking themselves how they ended up sitting in a room with no doors feeling like some sucker after the circus left town.

The unhappy folks who are still sitting at the table (more likely associates now than the partners who got the ball rolling) aren't talking about how much more money they can put to work; they're trying to figure out how little additional cash they've got to put up in order to preserve what's left of their position. Everyone is telling you that they're really not inclined to do much of anything at all if you can't drag some new money from outside players to the table to help set the price and get the next round started. Flat valuations in times like this are the new "up" rounds and there are down rounds galore. (See http://www.inc.com/howard-tullman/tech-startups-take-the-money-and-build.html.)

This is a Plan B world at best and the down and dirty talk on the limo ride to LaGuardia almost always includes whether to also shoot the CEO while they're in the process of trying to clean things up and save a little face. So if you're the one on the bubble, forget Plan B, and get started on what I call Plan C. You need to get a head start on talking about the tough choices and critical changes that need to be made. It's about figuring out what immediate actions you can take that will make a difference before they turn the lights out. You can have results or excuses, not both. Focus on facts rather than futures if you want to be around when things turn around. And forget about playing the blame game – no one cares.

Plan C is all about choices: contraction, consolidation, combination, conversion, and concessions. The last C is closing the doors and that's not a sight that anyone wants to see. So see which of the C's makes the most sense for your startup.

1. Contraction

Just suck it up and admit it. You can't be all things to all people and no one ever has been. Focus on what sets you apart and what represents the best prospect of a long-term sustainable competitive advantage for your business and forget everything else. Don't apologize, don't try to explain, just buckle down and get the job done. The recent launch of UberEats in Chicago (as an "instant" meal delivery service) and its almost immediate abandonment of that commitment is a good example of knowing when to hold 'em and when to fold 'em. It doesn't take a genius to figure out that it's pretty stupid to open the umpteenth home meal delivery service in Grub Hub's hometown.

Businesses that scale too soon and which are a mile wide and an inch deep are doomed for many reasons, but the clearest and most telling is that they can't cost-effectively engage with, support, or connect to their customers because the customers are simply too few and too far between. It's critical to nail it before you scale it and, if you're grossly over-extended, your business is going nowhere.

2. Consolidation

Shut down the stupid San Francisco office sooner rather than later. You had no business being there in the first place and the fact that you're doing no business there ought to speak for itself. San Francisco may be the most overheated and least representative market in America. Everyone there drinks the Kool-Aid for about 10 minutes and then moves on. Building a new business there is as slippery and unstable as trying to nail Jell-O to a tree.

New York should be next on the list. NYC isn't a city – it's 5 or 6 different marketplaces all mashed together – with a million people just waiting to eat your lunch. Your business expansion needs to be driven by actual demand, feasibility and real opportunities – not by some investor's fantasies and/or by fables about life in the Big Apple foisted on the public by the media and promoted by people barely making it in Brooklyn.

3. Combination

Take a careful look around and see who else in your space (or adjacent to it) is doing things right and see what the prospects of some kind of combination may be - especially if your market itself continues to become more cluttered and competitive. We hear constantly that the shared/surplus economy or the "Now" economy continues to grow fueled by millions of millennials holding multiple jobs. But tracking the gig economy isn't quite that easy. While the number of multiple job holders has in fact grown dramatically, the percentage of the number of people so employed as compared to the total number employed has been flat or down over the last decade. No one knows for sure what the new world of work will look like in a few years.

We had a great example of a timely and smart combination recently in Chicago where *Shiftgig* (www.shiftgig.com) and *BookedOut* (www.bookedout.com) got together and decided that there were all kinds of economies and opportunities in a merger as well as the sheer relief in knowing that they could stop trying to beat each other's brains out in the market. They are both players in the increasingly-crowded space which the Commerce Department is trying to define as "digital matching firms". *Shiftgig* was bigger and better established, but *BookedOut* had a lot of momentum and was gaining important traction in the experiential marketing sector. Now instead of spending time building duplicative back ends and other redundant systems and offerings, they can bring a single story to the market in a cleaner, more efficient and less costly way. This is exactly the kind of story that all of their investors wanted to hear.

It's not easy in any market to attract the technical talent, the motivated sales people, and the operations folks that you need to grow quickly. A well-planned and thoughtfully executed combination can demonstrably accelerate the process. You need to be careful to make sure that the companies' visions are aligned and that the problems they're addressing are similar and that the cultures of the businesses (and the leaders in particular) aren't in conflict. These things aren't made or broken in the board room when the papers are signed; they rise or fail in the implementation and the execution. But in today's world, it's often a lot better and smarter to combine than trying to go it alone.

4. Conversion

Sell some of your stuff to someone else. You may be great at lead generation and lousy at closing the sale once those prospects show up at your door. Or you may be a great sales organization that sucks at fulfillment and customer service. When you look at your skill sets and your customers, users, clients, etc. through a different lens – looking at them as potential assets to be converted or sold to some other enterprise - it helps you see more clearly exactly what kind of business you're building. It may make the most sense to look at your company as a conduit or an intermediary and not as a one-stop shop trying to meet all the needs of the marketplace. You've got to play to your strengths and build on those if you're planning to stick around.

5. Concessions

Maybe your pricing made sense in some early fever dream where you were the best and only player in the space, but now there are fast followers and clones everywhere you look and their offerings (at least on the surface) look a lot like yours. Once your customers start talking about price, you're on a very slippery slope. (See http://www.builtinchicago.org/blog/no-one-wins-race-bottom.)

Here's the bottom line. In the long run, you can't save your way to success and it's no fun to fire your friends or postpone your pet projects. But if you don't survive during the difficult times, you and your business won't be around to savor any success down the road. Do what needs to be done and do it now.

SCALE SMART - TAKE YOUR TIME - PICK YOUR SPOTS

I must have heard the story about the tortoise and the hare a few million times in my youth and you'd think I'd be sick of it by now. But - and this is amazing to me in today's "everything in a hurry" world - the basic lesson - that slow and steady progress wins the race in the long run - is still remarkably relevant and applicable - especially to new businesses. It sounds a little old fashioned and even a bit boring and it's rarely something that you'll hear any VC say - especially when the topic on the table is how quickly to scale the business, but it's something that the very best entrepreneurs always take to heart and keep top of mind. Rushing to roll out your business nationwide (and being a mile wide and an inch deep) may make the boys in the board room happy, but it's bad for your business if you aren't ready.

One of our recent Chicago success stories is *SpotHero* (www.spothero.com) which helps drivers find off-street parking spaces and owners fill their parking lots and garages. There couldn't be a better example of the "go slow until you get it right" approach. While competitors, copycats and other knock-offs attempted rapid geographic expansions across the country, *SpotHero* hunkered down and stayed in Chicago for the first two years of its existence. They figured out that you've got to nail it before you can scale it.

Today, 5 years later, they're still only in about 20 cities (with 5 major cities contributing about 98% of all their revenue), while one of the few competitors who are still standing is "doing business" in more than 150 cities. I say "doing business" because *SpotHero* earns more parking revenue in one of its cities than those guys do in all 150 of their cities combined. *SpotHero* is larger and growing faster than its remaining competitors (notwithstanding having raised less capital) because they continue to focus on deeper and better connections to each of their markets and customers rather than simply trying to be everywhere at once. Doing a lot of things is not the same as getting things done and done right.

Adding marginal inventory (or any other kinds of commitments) in new markets without assuring the presence of matching demand is an easy trip to the toilet. It's like the busted-out guy who takes an Uber to Bankruptcy Court and then invites the *Uber* driver into the proceedings as a creditor. Similarly, the kind of parking you're identifying and booking for the consumers who are using your services matters as well. Events parking is relatively easy, but it's also infrequent and a relatively small part of the overall market. *SpotHero* targeted the biggest and best parking concerns and locations in the country (with massive numbers of consistent- often daily – users) from the get-go and now works with 9 of the top 11 players including all 5 of the largest parking companies in the U.S.

It's never easy going after and trying to sign all the big guys. They're tougher and smarter and more demanding, but they're also the best businessmen. What you can learn from them and what they can help you accomplish is priceless. (See http://www.inc.com/howard-tullman/a-big-customer-wants-exclusivity-now-what.html .) If you can lock these folks in and deliver the right results for them, there's no better place to be and no easier way to scale. Let the other guys drive themselves crazy chasing Mom-and-

Perspiration Principles XX

Pop lots all over the place. What they're missing is that every new lot they add reduces the yield to the guys who came before and that Ponzi-ish approach can't make anyone very happy over time.

There are almost always at least two economic sides to any marketplace (regulators, legislators, etc. don't count for these purposes). When you're growing your new business, you need to be very careful in the process that you don't leave the early adopters and your beginning boosters behind. They were there for you when the whole thing got started and they're critical references, foundational supporters, and concrete demonstrations that your product or service is sticky. Tracking and driving improvements in same store sales are the best and easiest way to measure stickiness and the best way to keep score as well especially when those critical numbers keep ticking up year over year in your oldest markets. This is because, if the older customers lose interest or cashflow and they're leaking out of the back door, it doesn't matter how you're doing in terms of growing or buying new customers at the front end of the funnel. (See http://www.inc.com/howard-tullman/why-your-best-new-customers-are-your-old-customers.html.)

Good business isn't usually about beating the other guys - there will always be new and different competitors - and there will always be people pitching cheaper and even better solutions. Chasing someone else or trying to quickly copy their plans and trying to outdo them assumes that they know what they're doing and are a lot smarter than you. I don't think there's any good reason to believe that. Sustainable businesses create real, demonstrable value for their clients and customers and they keep upping the ante.

No one new gets to rest on their laurels or their past performance even if they have a track record to point to which most startups don't. Customers' expectations are progressive. It's NOT about how fast you're going (but never slow down), it's about how fast you're getting faster and better. It's all about acceleration, not simply velocity. And it's about innovative techniques and technologies rather than tonnage as well. Precision trumps sheer volume. Your pitches, programs and proposals must be better, not just longer or louder.

It's not always a discussion or a conversation about a specific contest, feature, function or challenge. As often as not - it's about making this discipline of "always trying to be a better you" a part of your company's culture and embedding it in the ways that you do business whether you're selling products or services - widgets or wisdom - or whatever.

Having a great product isn't enough. No one sells just a product these days. We're all in service businesses trying to secure not a single sale, but to grab and hang on to the lifetime value of each customer. Creating a business that will last is about building long-term relationships and compounding customer trust. Connection and continuing engagement coupled with constant improvement and innovation are what keeps you in the game. I wouldn't be surprised to see them developing some new tools soon which will let their lot owners dynamically price parking in their lots based on all the same kinds of variables that so many other services are now using for surge pricing.

Startups don't have an established following or a brand to rely upon as shorthand for their promise to deliver and/or as a way to overcome the decision fatigue that plagues all of us these days in a world of infinite choices. Startups make a future promise and then it's directly on them to deliver on their commitments and to keep raising the bar. It's your business's job to earn and retain my loyalty. Loyalty today means nothing more than the absence of a better alternative.

Over-promising and under-delivering is obviously fatal over time. And even the coolest technology alone won't get the job done. *SpotHero* stuck with old-fashioned paper documentation until they precisely figured out the needs, comfort levels and the concerns

Perspiration Principles XX

of their customers (for the moment) and – only then – did they build a killer mobile app that now handles more than 80% of their reservations. The other players are still using websites.

Bottom line: People don't long remember who was first; they only know who's best. *SpotHero*'s the best in the biz.

WHERE WILL YOUR BUSINESS BE WHEN THE MUSIC STOPS?

Do they still let kids play the "Musical Chairs" game or is it no longer politically correct? You know, that's the game where the players walk around a group of chairs to music and try to sit down quickly when the music abruptly stops. The challenge is that there is always one less chair than the number of players and the one left standing is eliminated. I've always loved it because of its metaphorical power as much as anything else. Building a new business (or a career) is a competitive race in many ways and – especially as you progress – you quickly learn that there's not always room at the table for everyone. I like to say that it's lonely at the top, but at least it's not crowded. Having our kids get a little slice of real life experience early on and come to understand that occasionally you might have to push or shove your way to a seat in order to succeed isn't the worst thing in the world for anyone.

My position on schools, teachers and parents who promote the "everyone's a winner and trophies all around" view of the world is very clear. I think they're killing our country's competitiveness and mortgaging our kids' future with a bunch of fake, feel-good, psychology that mainly lets everyone save face. And I'm not talking solely about the games they play – it's the same problem in the classroom as it is on the playing field. It's so much easier to administer and grade a useless multiple choice test and to inflate every kids' grades for their college applications than it is to create challenging course work and content that excites and engages them. (See http://www.inc.com/howard-tullman/stop-promoting-mediocrity-in-our-schools.html.)

Most teachers today are doing a crappy job of teaching our kids the critical thinking and problem-solving skill sets that it's going to take for them to succeed in the new digital and global economy. And too many parents are just too busy or otherwise occupied to take an active interest and role in their kids' educations. It's much simpler to just pat your kid on the head for "trying" than it is to sit and pour over his or her homework to see what they're learning. (See http://www.inc.com/howard-tullman/startup-lessons-for-kids-and-entrepreneurs.html.)

So, you can readily understand why I would wonder if Musical Chairs is just another "too real" contest whose time has come and gone. But, for me, it's also an everyday reminder of a very critical fact of life for startups that we all need to keep in mind. Most startups aren't going to grow up to be stand-alone big businesses. A few of the best ones will find a way to get there. (See http://www.inc.com/howard-tullman/protect-your-startup-from-big-competitors.html.) But most young businesses are going to need some serious shelter from the coming storms and they're going to have to plan to fold their product or service into someone's else's success story.

There's always a lot of talk about how technology is a "winner take all" business and it's not wrong, it's just a tad overstated. Because there's so much money sloshing around these days to fund competitors and because I think we're going to see a likely return to more government antitrust oversight, we're much more likely to have strong oligopolies (2 or 3 main winners) rather than monopolies in most tech-driven markets. This is slightly better news for growing startups because it increases the pool of prospective buyers. But it's still going to be a tough road. And the early signs are already starting to show.

1. We've had it up to here with additional apps.

Downloads of new apps are dropping every month and the trend is accelerating. The glut is growing and - for a new entrant - it's virtually impossible to be found among the 50,000 new offerings pouring into the app stores each month. And, in case it isn't obvious, if you can't be found, you will never be chosen. In addition, we're lazy and we're digital creatures of habit so we barely use the vast majority of the apps already on our phones. If we were better housekeepers and tossed some of these unused apps, our screens would be a lot cleaner and we'd save tons of time that's now lost searching for specific icons lurking somewhere in the mess. At best, we're using maybe 5 to 7 apps a month on any kind of consistent basis and, according to *comScore*, 50% of our activity is concentrated on a single (usually social) app. If you're a standalone app, you'd better start looking for a home.

2. We're gravitating to do-it-all gateways, not dedicated gadgets.

Fitbit is flailing. Retailers are flooded with product sitting on their shelves and that makes huge Xmas orders for additional product highly problematic. How many wrists do they think we have? How many measurements really matter to most of us? And how many dedicated devices does anyone want or need when each and every day the basic functionality (steps, heart rate, BP, etc.) is being built right into all of our other mobile devices? And *Fitbit*'s caught in a classic squeeze from both ends of the price spectrum which is likely to persist. *Apple* wants to own the high end and *Xiaomi* is chipping away at the lower end of the range. But there's a much bigger structural problem facing all the gadget guys.

We are a country of one-stop shoppers and it's the folks that control the gateways, the channels and the top-of-mind interfaces, not the gadgets, who are increasingly becoming the only games in town. No one is better at this game right now than *Facebook*. (See http://www.inc.com/howard-tullman/facebooks-fabulous-future.html.) Honestly, it's only a matter of time before it becomes clear that all the tracking devices, all the navigation devices, all the data-generating wearables of whatever stripe (just like all the content created by professional media publishers) will need to knuckle under and feed their results thru Facebook's front door to the consumer because that's where the consumer lives and that's where the data needs to be. Facebook's phone was a bust, but guess what? They figured out a better and far more profitable way to serve their users and they shifted all the risk, pain and costs of production onto the backs of the gadget guys. If you're a dedicated device, not made by *Apple*, or in bed already with *Facebook*, you're toast.

3. We've decided that good enough is more than enough for most of us.

GoPro is gasping. Competition is up, diversification into drones is going nowhere fast, Christmas looks lousy, and the forecast for the year is down. And they're having a hard time manufacturing the next new thing. Sounds just like the litany of *Fitbit*'s woes. The truth is that most of us are mere mortals and we don't need the newest and greatest anything - we just need something in our price range to get the job done. And the competition is pushing the prices down and the basic quality up. In almost every tech sector, the players keep raising the bar and upping the average so that, in most cases, good enough today is plenty for the vast majority of customers. *GoPro* has

Perspiration Principles XX

burned through the pros, the enthusiasts, and the super-picky (and price-insensitive) people and now they're staring into the consumer chasm and facing a world of competitors (including all the phone manufacturers) whose offerings keep getting better, cheaper and more waterproof. It's hard at this point to imagine what they would call their sustainable competitive advantage. If you're the price and quality leader in your space, you need to start working on Plan B.

And overall, regardless of where you feel you fall, now's the right time to take a hard look at just what you have and what you've built and to sit down with your team and your advisors and discuss what the best alternatives are to capture and extract whatever value you've created in the business before it goes away. It's already past time in most cases (and largely a waste of time) to talk about how anyone is going to recoup their prior investments as opposed to their pro rata share of today's value. No one who's interested in moving forward spends much time looking in the rearview mirror. They call these kinds of dollars "sunk costs" for a very good reason. They're long gone and they're not coming back.

DON'T BLAME THE DATA FOR THE DEBACLE

Recent newspaper headline: "How Data Failed Us in Calling An Election". Here's a flash – it wasn't the data's fault – it was the media's mess. I realize that the search for someone or something else to blame is always successful; but I think it's abundantly clear who was really responsible for the situation. It was the prognosticators and the professional blowhards who got it so wrong. The truth is that the data doesn't know or care. It's like the Dude in *The Big Lebowski* – it simply abides. What you do with it and how it's used makes all the difference. If you let a monkey drive your car, it's not the monkey's fault when the accidents and crashes come.

So let's not dump on the data and data-driven decision making (which is essential to the future of almost every business) just because a bunch of over-eager media messiahs ignored the science, misapplied the mechanisms, and tried to manufacture a true miracle out of a mess of mixed messages which were never going to accurately predict the ultimate voting behaviors of millions of people who weren't prepared to share their true feelings with anyone and especially not with paid political pollsters with an agenda and the answers they claimed to be seeking already firmly fixed in their minds.

The most basic breakdown in the "research" process this time around was the fact that the pollsters weren't looking impartially for information; they were simply seeking confirmation and affirmation of what they wanted to see and hear using a deeply-flawed system and a methodology that everyone knows is meaningless in today's mobile and digital world. Just another ugly byproduct of the world of cable news where we only watch and listen to the people who tell us what we want to hear. It's the worst possible combination of an echo chamber in which you sit drinking your own *Kool-Aid*.

If you use a screwdriver to slice your roast beef, who exactly do you think is to blame for the chunky cuts that result and which end up looking totally disgusting and pre-chewed? Is it really the tool's fault? Maybe you should have used a Phillips instead of a flathead for a more presentable platter. Or maybe you should have taken a moment to think about whether the instrument you chose would ever be up to the task that you set out to accomplish. The heaviest hammer still can't nail Jell-O to a tree. We should really know by now and freely admit that no amount of historical information is likely to accurately predict certain kinds of human behaviors. Voting isn't the same as buying a vacuum cleaner – you never know what the voters will do until after they've done it.

In much the same way, if a major part of your prospective voter polling methodology is predicated on calling large parts of a population that no longer answers their phones or which has a substantial cohort under a certain age that doesn't even own a landline phone any longer; what would lead you to believe that you had any real basis to believe your results or that they were probative or predictive of anything that mattered?

And this is the situation even before you factor in the really depressing fact that the people desperate enough to waste their time talking to strangers on the phone are as likely as not to tell those folks exactly what they think they want to hear or what passes for the politically correct answers of the day rather than how they really feel or plan to vote. The telephone is maybe the worst possible tool for eliciting the truth about anything. Political research calls are the second most dreaded calls you can get these days – only PBS pledge drive calls are worse.

But based on the self-serving and misguided <u>mea culpas</u> that we're reading and hearing these days in and from every major media outlet, they did their very level best to bring you the correct stories and you'd think that those rascally polling numbers underlying the breathlessly reported trends that seemed to change from minute to minute must have had a mind of their own and gone way way off the reservation and miles from the last remnants of reality. The people who can't dance always blame the band for playing the wrong music.

The truth is that the numbers are neutral at best (except when they're just dead wrong as in some of the state polls) and the data's not to blame when it's tortured and twisted in support of answers and expected behaviors that it was never capable of predicting in the first place. It reminds me of a thermos – it doesn't really know whether it's keeping some beverage hotter or cooler for a period of time – it just sits there and does its job.

If we want explanations or excuses for the fact that the folks who were supposed to know didn't know anything in the end – we have to look at them (the number crunchers) – not the numbers. They're happy to have all of the responsibility; it's only fair – given the results - that they have a full share of the blame as well.

MAKE YOUR MEETINGS "CRISP" OR FORGET THEM

It's not possible these days to read any new or old material about organizational behavior without coming across a screed or two on the general subject of how too many meetings simply represent a waste of time, energy and resources. I've also written here on aspects of the same issue. (See http://www.inc.com/howard-tullman/how-to-deal-with-time-wasters.html.) These sessions rarely accomplish anything except maybe some pseudo-bonding; they don't have a logical and clearly-understood endpoint so they seem both pointless and endless; and, most often, they sorta drool to a conclusion without agreed-upon action items and/or documented next steps for at least half the people in the room.

Maybe holding meetings for meetings sake makes the miserable managers feel more productive, but they don't do much of anything for the business but waste a bunch of time. If the people in the meeting really had a choice, they'd rather eat dirt than sit through another moment of time in their life that they'll never get back to help justify someone else's job security. Managers who don't already (and always) have a pretty good idea and a solid handle on what their folks are doing or about to do (and why) aren't doing their own jobs.

Unfortunately, every business these days - regardless of age or size - seems to suffer from this syndrome and it doesn't appear to be getting any better. I even see it every day walking around 1871 and peering into our many conference rooms where two seconds of checking peoples' postures will tell you the whole sad story. Are they engaged and leaning in, are they actively contributing to the discussion, or are they just leaning back and shooting the breeze? And, of course, the worst cases of all are those where you see the alleged leaders of the meeting (who're supposed to be running the show) sprawled all over the place like a bag of spilled and soiled laundry. Watching the last remnants of any energy seeping slowly out of these unwitting captives sitting sadly in their chairs is truly depressing. I'd rather watch paint dry.

These kinds of make-work meetings are a menace to every company's momentum. They swiftly suck the oxygen and the urgency out of whatever initiatives and good ideas might be floating around. They're poorly planned, badly organized and run, and grudgingly attended by most of the participants who sit slouched in their seats trying to look engaged or trying to sneak a peek at their phones. The only people who really enjoy these sessions are those seeking a respite from doing any real work and - as a result - they're more than content to sit silently in some corner and just focus on keeping their eyes open. (See http://www.inc.com/howard-tullman/trying-to-motivate-your-employees-forget-it.html .)

Frankly, any recurring staff or team meetings (especially kick-off meetings for the week) that take more than 30 minutes are probably over-populated; attempting to cover a bunch of unnecessary stuff; giving everyone a chance to chat so we don't hurt their feelings; and otherwise driven by some foolish need to justify the time spent by the attendees in getting to the meeting. Here's a flash – the shorter the meeting, the more people that will thank you – regardless of the length of their journey. Everyone's got better things to be doing.

Perspiration Principles XX

Sharing important and timely information in regular update sessions only makes sense if every participant consciously edits their input and if some of them - from time to time - are smart and courageous enough to pass entirely instead wasting everyone's time with a useless report or a compulsory comment. Not every department is doing something every week that honestly matters to the whole team.

Here's a simple rule of thumb for when to keep your own mouth shut – don't say a thing unless it's going to help someone else in the room do their job better. Otherwise, stifle the urge and save us all from hearing how you spent your weekend or plan to spend the week ahead. Trying to keep everyone in the loop on everything is a game for losers and a major time suck. You want your people turned on - not tired out - especially as you start out the week.

I think the key is to keep the meetings that you absolutely must have as "CRISP" as you can.

<u>Concise:</u>More than a couple of topics is simply too much – focus on a few important things.

<u>Rigorous:</u> Keep everyone on the case - start with questions – end with answers and action items.

<u>Immediate:</u> What needs to be done well right now – push off the stuff that can wait a while.

<u>Short:</u> Not one minute more than you need – no need to fill the time with fluff or folderol.

<u>Prompt:</u> Start and end on time – every time – and let the latecomers watch from the wings.

WISE WORDS FROM THE WITCH IN WICKED

Who would have thought that there would be some worthwhile words of wisdom coming from Glinda, the Good Witch, in *Wicked*? I saw *Wicked* again recently for the umpteenth time and I was struck by how relevant some of the lyrics from the song "Thank Goodness" were to the entrepreneurial mindset and to the ways many entrepreneurs behave. These pithy but poignant phrases were words that any struggling entrepreneur would recognize. And they were so timely as well, given that Thanksgiving is right around the corner, when we're all supposed to be so aggressively appreciative.

One of the things that we entrepreneurs don't do well is to say "thank you" fast enough or often enough to so many of the people that matter in our lives and who make our achievements possible. Not just thanks to our peers and team members, but to our friends, family, investors, advisors and mentors as well. Why is that and why can't we do better? Of course, this could be a function of busy schedules and the fact that we're all in a hurry these days – although it's not actually that hard to be thankful and to take a minute or two to let someone know that you are – so that seems like a somewhat inadequate explanation. Praise and recognition are quick, easy and cost-effective ways to acknowledge and reward your people's contributions. And worth making time for. Success is definitely sweeter when it is shared.

But the truth is that there are some deeper-seated startup psychologies at work and, while these aren't offered as excuses, at least they're a plausible explanation for some behaviors that don't otherwise make much personal or business sense. Frankly, entrepreneurs just aren't that conscientious about taking the time to say "thanks" to the people who helped them along the way. But I honestly don't think that this behavior is because most of us are unappreciative or simply ingrates.

I think it's more that we're uncomfortable and don't quite know how to handle these circumstances when we're thrust into the spotlight. Celebrations are so yesterday. They make you feel like your goals are behind you and that's just not how entrepreneurs look at the world. So we tend to clam up and try to soldier through the ceremonies, but our heads aren't really in the game. We're somewhat awkward, completely stuck in our own minds, and maybe a little tongue-tied in these cases because – in some respects – we just don't believe or buy into the whole process and we're a little surprised to find ourselves in such a spot. It's a little hard to be gracious when your principal goal is to get off the stage.

In the *Wicked* play, Glinda is supposed to be joyously celebrating her engagement, but, as things progress and she sings about how "happy" she is, we hear more and more of a tone that suggests that she's got some very mixed feelings about what's going on around her. According to the crowd and the conventional wisdom, her "dreams" have all come true, but she's not so sure. She says that "**it is, I admit, the tiniest bit unlike I anticipated**".

And, instead of being a happy and simple time, "**getting your dreams – it's strange, but it seems a little – well – complicated.**" She knows that she should be overjoyed and grateful, but she's not quite there yet. We've all been in similar circumstances – waiting for someone to pinch us to make sure things are real. And it's also a bit of the "dog that caught the car" syndrome. You finally grabbed the brass ring that you've been chasing for a while. Now what? And maybe even more importantly, you find yourself – just like Glinda - wondering what you had to give up in the process to get there.

Most of the best entrepreneurs I know would tell you that they do a lot better in tough times and in dealing with adversity than they do with success and when things are working out well. Success is a little like wine. It's just hard for a true entrepreneur to believe in it. You don't believe in wine. You drink it, enjoy it for a moment, and then you try to get on with your life. Entrepreneurs are superstitious and they want to get back to work before anyone notices and before anyone can snatch the moment away. For a lot of us who are confirmed paranoids, these "celebrations" are rarely joyous occasions. At best, they're waystations on what we expect to be a much longer and harder road ahead.

It also has something to do with authenticity as every returning vet will tell you. Only the guys actually in the trenches – the entrepreneurs themselves – really know how close to the line things got – how near to the edge they came – and how much luck (and even a little fear) had to do with the outcome. And only the entrepreneur knows all the sacrifices that it took to get there and how quickly these things can turn around and race in the wrong direction. Glinda says: "**There's a kind of a sort of a cost. There's a couple of things get lost. There are bridges you cross you didn't know you crossed until you've crossed.**" These things are hard to share with folks who haven't been there.

And then there's this crazy idea that has you asking yourself exactly how big a deal it could be if you (of all people) were able to pull it off. It's a little hard to congratulate and thank your teammates when you're not sure whether you even deserve the credit in the first place. The battle's always far from over, there's no finish line – just another hill, and it's a lot more like sitting on tacks than it is resting on your laurels.

The world thinks that most entrepreneurs are beyond confident, if not arrogant, but the truth is that they're mostly scared little guys running full speed ahead, jumping over the potholes, and trying to look over both their shoulders to see who's coming up behind them to take their toys away.

Is it any wonder that they forget from time to time to say thank you for the honor?

THE POOR I.T. GUYS CAN ONLY TIE

I used to feel bad for the guys in our IT department because they had the same lifetime problem that the heads of Homeland Security have. As we all know, the terrorists and other scumbags only have to get it right one time and horrible things can happen while our counter-terrorism teams and other law enforcement personnel have to try to be right every time and then – when nothing happens – no one bothers to give them any thanks or other recognition. People just whine about the costs, the delays, and the stupid rules and figure that protecting us is what we're paying these folks to do. The best the good guys can hope for is a tie. No harm, no foul and sadly no credit for keeping us safe.

I think that the IT departments in almost every business have been similarly taken for granted (or given the Rodney Dangerfield "no respect" treatment) and they get little or no recognition from anyone even though the complexity, significance and risks associated with their responsibilities in our companies' operations have multiplied geometrically in the last decade. You basically can't do anything intelligent today in almost any business without solid, timely, reliable and accurate data – it's the oil of the digital age – and the IT guys are the ones with their mitts on the meters, mechanisms and measurements – the IT infrastructures – that are the make-or-break gates, tools and tunnels through which everything critical in our data-driven world passes. If they don't get it right, your business simply doesn't get done and – relative to your competition – you might as well be back in the Dark Ages.

So I've been spending a fair amount of time talking to and coaching IT teams (as well as working with smart startups which are developing new approaches to help cut through the clutter in big corporations so the data can efficiently get through to the people and places it needs to be) and I'm encouraged to see a few positive signs and a slowly-growing acknowledgement of the importance, the criticality and the severity of the problems to which under-investing and under-appreciating the centrality of your IT team exposes your entire company. We humans only understand the degree of our dependence on these machines and systems (which dictate so much of our lives today) when the devices shut down, the data disappears, and the systems stop delivering the information we need to proceed.

And while you can say that time eventually changes everything, the truth is that time only changes (usually for the worse) what you don't change first. I tell all the IT people that I meet that they have to be their own best advocates and change agents and act on their own behalf if they really want to see meaningful improvements and add real value to their businesses. This is no easy sell because these folks aren't really built that way and "selling" their ideas is the last thing they ever thought they'd be stuck doing. The waves of change are coming – you can swim with the tides or sit still and be submerged.

I've found that there are three specific ideas and approaches that senior-level IT folks need to focus on if they want to make a serious contribution to the future of their firms.

1. Be a Weapon, not a Shield

Playing great defense isn't enough these days and the smartest IT players are the ones turning the data they're developing and extracting from the deluge of connected devices into "weaponized" information and decision tools that move their businesses ahead by providing better and more timely solutions to both internal users and outside customers and clients. What gets measured is what gets done and comprehensive measurement – that tracks installation <u>and</u> adoption <u>and</u> improved outcomes – is all a necessary part of getting smarter. Helping your team optimize every aspect of your operations by giving them real-time decision support puts them in a position to make the most critical calls – like when they should double down on their winners and how soon to ditch the dogs – quickly and correctly. Triage is crucial because no one has unlimited resources today and enabling cost-effective execution by providing increased metrics and visibility is what the best data-driven IT strategies are all about. Money is just expendable ammunition – data is power – and guess who's in charge of the data?

2. Focus on the Future, Stop Patching Up the Past

Everything is about the future and we need bridges forward and not just more bandages. (See http://www.inc.com/howard-tullman/build-a-bridge-over-your-old-code-not-another-band-aid-.html.) The network is the name of the game and helping your team exploit the extensive resources outside of your own shop is essential. Connecting your company to the critical partners, collaborators, and new technologies that are outside your four walls (and doing so securely without sacrificing speed, accuracy or ease of access) is the most pressing challenge. Equally crucial is to make sure that your people are an active and effective part of all the "social" conversations that concern your business (but don't necessarily invite or include you) because these new channels are changing the way we all confer, compare, communicate and consume. If your products and services are part of the ongoing conversations and apart of the decision set when the buyers are ready to buy, you're nowhere. Finally, holding down the fort just isn't enough; you've got to do more than simple maintenance because your business needs a vision and a path forward – not another Mr. Fix-It.

3. Make Sure You're in "The Room Where It Happens"

If you don't ask, you don't get. As a senior IT professional, you've got to step up and insist that your presence and your input is central to securing the best solutions for the business. There's a great song in the play *Hamilton* about the importance of being in "the room where it happens" – where the decisions are made that impact us all – and if you're not there – if you don't have some skin in the game – if you just a spectator standing around and waiting – then the changes that do happen will happen to you – not through you. It's not always safe to step up – it's never about security or the status quo – but it's the smartest bet you can make. If you don't believe in yourself and your abilities, who else will? And take my word for it, waiting never gets you to a better result because the world is just moving too quickly to give anyone the luxury of time. Just like in racing, you need to understand that no one waits for you.

If it's any consolation in these tough and troubling times, just remember that they're going to blame you for anything and everything that goes wrong anyway. So, if you're already walking on thin ice, you might as well dance.

ABOUT THE AUTHOR

Howard Tullman is the CEO of 1871 in Chicago where digital startups get their start. He is also the General Managing Partner of two venture funds: Chicago High-Tech Investment Partners and G2T3V, LLC, which both focus on funding disruptive innovators. He is the former Chairman and CEO of Tribeca Flashpoint Media Arts Academy in Chicago. He is an active member of numerous city, state and civic boards and organizations and a tireless supporter and mentor to many start-ups and other businesses and individuals. He has successfully founded more than a dozen high-tech businesses in his 50 year career and created more than $1 billion in investor value as well as thousands of new jobs. He writes a regular weekly blog on The Perspiration Principles for Inc. Magazine and can be directly contacted:

- by email at h@1871.com
- on twitter @tullman
- his blog: tullman.blogspot.com
- his primary website: www.tullman.com

To get all of Howard's blog posts in one download, visit Blogintobook.com/tullman/.

www.ingramcontent.com/pod-product-compliance
Lightning Source LLC
Chambersburg PA
CBHW061222180526
45170CB00003B/1121